THE YELLOW HEART

El corazón amarillo

PABLO NERUDA

The Yellow Heart

TRANSLATED BY WILLIAM O'DALY

COPPER CANYON PRESS : PORT TOWNSEND

Publication of this book was made possible by a grant
from the National Endowment for the Arts.
Copper Canyon Press is in residence with Centrum
at Fort Worden State Park.
ISBN 1-55659-028-8 (cloth)
ISBN 1-55659-029-6 (paper)
Library of Congress Catalog Number 89-81834
Cover monotype by Galen Garwood
The type is Sabon, set by The Typeworks, Vancouver, B.C.

Second Printing

COPPER CANYON PRESS
Post Office Box 271
Port Townsend, Washington 98368

CONTENTS

TRANSLATOR'S ACKNOWLEDGMENTS

There is no way to adequately thank my friend Michael Constans for his generosity with his knowledge of the Spanish and English languages. His discriminating ear for the original poems helped to "bridge the notes." I am grateful to the Spanish language editor at Copper Canyon Press, Stephanie Lutgring, for her expertise and grace. Tom Dean, Shelley Means, and Lynn Guthrie offered various forms of moral and editorial support; and with her belief and a certain pen, I have been honored by Nancy Jacobs. My astute colleagues in International once again provided helpful interpretations of the more ambiguous colloquialisms in the original manuscript. The commitment of Copper Canyon Press, specifically Tree Swenson, Sam Hamill, and Mary Jane Knecht, to publishing this series of the late and posthumous poetry of Pablo Neruda has been unswerving and offered with a keen sensitivity to the needs of the project. In our evolving conversation on the nature of improvisation, my editor at Copper Canyon, Mr. Hamill, has offered insights that developed into the perspective I take on Neruda in the introduction. And since the beginning of this project fifteen years ago, I have benefited consistently from the encouragement and support of my family.

INTRODUCTION

The Improvisational Spirit of Pablo Neruda

Soon after they discover, book by book, that there are many Pablo Nerudas, his most avid readers come to see there is only one. The two-volume set of his collected works in Spanish, printed on onion-skin and not yet complete, runs close to three thousand pages. Given the remarkable range and diversity of his work, from early love poems and experiments in humanistic surrealism, to the historical and mythological *Canto General* and the odes to spoons and winter, to this playful and irreverent book, *The Yellow Heart* (1974), the Chilean Nobel Laureate quite clearly crafted his poems with numerous voices and a multitude of feet. In *Extravagaria*, Neruda tells the story from the inside:

> While I am writing, I'm far away;
> and when I come back, I've gone.
> I would like to know if others
> go through the same things that I do,
> have as many selves as I have,
> and see themselves similarly;
> and when I've exhausted this problem,
> I'm going to study so hard
> that when I explain myself,
> I'll be talking geography.

> ("We Are Many," *Extravagaria*)

What distinguishes Neruda's poetry is "composition impelled by knowledgeable spirit," a phrase coined by the poet Hayden Carruth to describe the nature of improvisation. In his writings on jazz, Carruth uses the word in a way most directly connected to its Latin root, *improvisus,* "to not foresee." In the context of poetry, the word suggests that the sensibility of the poet (his emotional, intellectual, and

7

spiritual history) engages the experience at hand in an impromptu dance. The dance develops organically, guided by thematic ideas established in the first few poems and then turned over and over, until those ideas come to an emotional and musical resolution. The final form of the poem derives from the content and is not foreseen, a perpetual surprise in the search for truth.

During most of his fifty years of publishing, Neruda came to have far more passion for the full improvisational life of the imagination than for its flashes of lightning or comfortable dwellings. Charles Baudelaire, an early influence on Neruda, argues in "Salon of 1859" that the imagination is "queen of the faculties" because it "decomposes all creation" and with the collected materials it "creates a new world." The process of making the poem gives back to nature all it had joined together, to produce "a new flowering and a strange music." These ideas describe the impulse for Neruda's evolution as a poet, and they circumscribe the same spiraling motion found in the work of jazz musicians and poets trained in the oral tradition.

> I am here while from sky to sky
> the shiver of migrating birds
> leaves me sunk in myself and in my flesh
> as in a deep well of perpetuity
> dug by a motionless spiral.
>
> ("The Triangles," *Winter Garden*)

In his search for organic form, Neruda turns through his set of personal symbols, obsessive themes, and basic rhythms of perception toward a new insight into the "structure of feeling" (Carruth). In that search, Neruda's craft continued to develop throughout his life — when he wrote poems, it was with his entire body and soul. He composed with a youthful and wizened sensibility shaped by the rainy forests outside Temuco, the raging and frozen rivers, and the rolling pastureland rising toward snowcapped Villarica. His intellect and heart were nourished by a tremendous curiosity about the physical and spiritual emanations of the natural world. And Neruda had committed himself and his work, at the outbreak of the Spanish Civil War, to satisfying the traditional responsibility of a "poet of the people": he would expose various forms of treachery that disrupt the balance of humanity's relationship with the world of the sea and the stars, and with itself. He encourages humanity to cease its abuses, yet he finds himself as culpable as everybody else. Struggling with that contradiction in *The Yellow Heart,* he sees himself as a "swindled naturalist" as well as a priest ordained in the orders of politics and love.

In this late book, Neruda revisits these obsessive themes with the eyes and ears of a consummate craftsman. In the process of discovering the tones given off by his autumnal heart, he frees himself from the voices he developed in the lyrical and political poetry. As Czeslaw Milosz has said, "Only if we assume that a poet constantly strives to liberate himself from borrowed styles in search of reality is he dangerous. In a room where people unanimously maintain a conspiracy of silence, one word of truth sounds like a pistol shot." Neruda spent the last forty years of his life making himself dangerous with his poetry and his activism, by responding to the realization that all people are one people.

He came to see poetry as a moral act, with personal and communal responsibilities. A poet's investiture is to remember where we came from and to ask who we are, to ask who we are as a community and where we are headed. When Neruda composed his poems, he gave himself to the process as if he were still the small boy in his own dream, surrounded at the family feast by gunfire and smoke, guitars and wine. In that dream, recalled in *Passions and Impressions,* he is dressed in black and holds a cup of still-warm lamb's blood to his lips – terrified, dying like the lamb and toasting to joy, he drinks the blood. The imagery represented for Neruda a willingness to accept his investiture as a human being and as a poet, whose anguish and joy derive from his response to the world.

From the beginning, Neruda was impelled to write poems "as

impure as a suit or a body, a poetry with wrinkles . . . declarations of love and hatred, beasts, blows, idylls, manifestos, denials, doubts, affirmations, taxes." He was successful at never adopting too narrow a prescription for the appropriate subject matter of poetry. He is as faithful to his experiences of absurdity and even melancholy ("that sentimentalism of another age") as he is to other sources of the poem more palatable to modern critics. For him, what is most important is to make the expression new (a position consistent with the theories of Jelly Roll Morton and Ezra Pound). The poem can then serve as a suitable home for truth, manifested in the present.

Neruda believed poetic form to be as dynamic as the processes of transformation and discovery. Form and content constantly shape each other, like the elements of an ecosystem, and this allows truth infinite possibilities for expression. He was aware that lyric poetry is a suspect genre, and as a consequence of our suspicion we sometimes apply narrow aesthetic principles to its composition. In *Passions and Impressions,* Neruda writes that "the mania for pedantry" in poetry casts aside certain marvels of the lyric: "moonlight, the swan at dusk, 'my beloved,' are, beyond question, the elemental and essential matter of poetry. He who would flee from bad taste is riding for a fall."

The diverse poems in *The Yellow Heart* — whether they are celebratory, allegorical, or oddly lyrical — declare the strong presence of Neruda's improvisational spirit. In an ironic way, it works as an element of consistency from poem to poem that (were there any question) marks this posthumously published volume as authentic. The first poem signals that he is returning to recapitulate the evolutionary elements of his poetic landscape. Referring to the needleworkers of the coastal village of Isla Negra, his favorite home during his final years, he writes:

> Because I am unfinished and spindle-shaped
> I had an understanding with needles
> and then they were threading me
> and never have finished.

That's why the love I give you,
my woman, my needle woman,
coils in your ear moistened
by the sea winds of Chillán
and uncoils in your eyes,
letting sadnesses drift.

("One," *The Yellow Heart*)

In *Passions and Impressions,* he acknowledges that the needle-workers may explain "why the roots of my poetry are deep in the soil of this place." They create him as they embroider "with the colored threads of blue innocence, violet profundity, red clarity . . . they embroider with the color of their hearts." Guitars, trains, elephants, and cherry trees are other lifelong personal symbols that return in the process of improvising the poem, and serve as intellectual and emotional points of navigation. For Neruda, the guitar is the South American lyre, the instrument that resonates in his voice, conjuring symbols from his childhood. The trains carry melancholy freight, steeped in contradictory emotions toward his stern but dedicated father, a railroad worker who took him on rides through the Andean foothills. Locomotives steam toward an undeclared destination or stand empty in the rain, moving ahead of us into the future or locked in the past, unattainable. And they never arrive at the same future we're destined for.

And I, in the train, like stale smoke,
with so many shiftless souls,
burdened by so many deaths,
felt myself lost on a journey
in which nothing was moving
but my exhausted heart.

("A Dream of Trains," *Extravagaria*)

And from his bestiary, the elephant is the poet himself, excessive in his pride and self-centered in love, who lifts his lover into the branches of a cherry tree with his trunk. These symbols and others appear in *The Yellow Heart* in a more personal way than before, without as much commentary or context, as in the poem "Disasters":

> But the gentle morning
> painted the black night blue
> and the enemy stars
> were swallowed by the light
> while I sang peacefully
> with no catastrophe and no guitar.

> ("Disasters," *The Yellow Heart*)

The thematic structure of *The Yellow Heart* can be represented as layered, or even prismatic: the more intimate the reader becomes with the poems, the more the yellow light of Neruda's waning years, with its irreverence and satirical humor, breaks into varying emotional hues and tones. That "yellow light," representative of the book's irreverence and sarcasm, is most evident in the poems that spoof manners and social customs, and in turn the poet's rebellion against them. It is also the source of much of the book's playfulness: the exaggerated situations of the nudist with a mission in "The Hero" and of the friend terrified of nightfall in "The Hieroglyphic Chicken." This is also true of the allegory about contemporary Latin American feudalism and internecine warfare called "Memories of Friendship" and the ghost story of the family in "An Untenable Situation," who sit around the fireplace all day recalling their dead.

Much of the humor is self-parody, as in "Precious Stone," a poem that blends darker tones with the humor. In this poem, the narrator puts the moves on a woman who reminds him of a cherry, beautiful and bursting with life. His approach has the distant ring of a traditional dandy's in that he ultimately is a victim of his vanity and pride in the expression of his individuality. In this case, he grows his nose, the tender object of her affection, into an inflated image of his libido. She quite understandably rejects his advances:

> I struggled to unroll
> my nose until it turned
> into an elephant's trunk.

With mortal sleights of hand
I took my skill to such a level
that I raised Precious Stone
to the branches of a cherry tree.

That woman rejected
my colossal tributes
and never came down from the branches:
she abandoned me. Afterwards I knew
that little by little, in time,
she turned into a cherry.

("Precious Stone," *The Yellow Heart*)

It is interesting to note that in *Twenty Love Poems and a Song of Despair* (1924), the poet wants to do with his lover "what spring does to the cherry trees." In "Precious Stone" fifty years later, he strives to make his romantic desire a reality, and though he tries and tries, there is nothing he can do to make her want him. His only recourse is to find a way to live with the painful paradox of un-requited love – she rejected him in spite of his efforts to exaggerate the part of his nature that he thought attracted her. It's the end of their relationship, not the springtime he expected. The poem can also be read as a good-natured assault on the Romantic idealization of the individual in an exaggerated manner reminiscent of Balzac: it's a paradox of being human that demands we must keep our pride, a prime source of our failings, in order to survive.

In the poem "Disasters," with metaphors based on volcanic eruptions and floods, Neruda catalogues images of the political chaos that ushered in the 1973 military coup and of his quiet life in Isla Negra. While assassins and reporters occupy the streets of Santiago, Neruda makes his bed "far from every city." At last he can sleep peacefully, settled into his favorite home on earth, but he is living in terror of a "malignant" star. This seems to be an allusion to the cancer inside him, as distant and real as a star. The pervasive quality of paradox and the star as a personal symbol of it both take something from the poetry of Charles Baudelaire. Both poets see physical objects as mysterious; they are the embodiment of paradox because in themselves they can never be decided or solved – they offer no answers. Our lives traverse the region that lies between opposites, and that tension is a catalyst in our lives. It determines in internal and external ways the experience of the poetry itself, with figures of speech and metaphors composed of correspondences between unlike things. In the correspondence, these things are uprooted from their meaning in order to signify something else, yet the new thing derives its definition from the original meanings. Another instance of this is the poet's use of allegory, where nothing is or stands for itself alone but rather functions as a relay for something else. The theme of paradox as implicit in experience is a preoccupation of Neruda's as early as the *Residencias,* with their vibrant images of motion at rest, energy simultaneously harnessed by and generated within a form.

While the world is falling apart around him, Neruda returns to two souls currently out of vogue in literary circles, in what seems to be a tongue-in-cheek statement of aesthetics. Both literary figures mentioned in the lines below influenced his sensibility as an adolescent, one now pigeon-holed as a necromantic lush and the other rarely taught or read in our minimalist age, if for no other reason than the sheer bulk of his "imperfect" classic.

> In Valparaíso the houses
> were falling around me
> and I ate breakfast in the wreckage
> of my lost library
> between a surviving Baudelaire
> and a dismantled Cervantes.
>
> ("Disasters," *The Yellow Heart*)

It is fitting that Baudelaire and Cervantes, as social misfits, should surface in a book rebelling against the conventions that make them appear crazy. And it's not surprising we would find Neruda, a dying man, returning to early and lasting influences. He translated

Baudelaire when he was a teenager; and his grade school teacher, Gabriela Mistral, exposed him to the classics of Spanish literature, including the irrepressible *Don Quixote*. Baudelaire and Cervantes suited and influenced particular parts of Neruda (who in many aspects of his poetry is also their antithesis). He admires Cervantes for the tremendous sweep of his tale, the collective life of his imagination, rather than for the perfection (or lack of it) of the details of his craftsmanship. The legacy of the knight errant or of a poet's oeuvre lives not in any single deed or inspired turn of phrase, but in the fact that it is a chosen life: it is founded upon a commitment to values and action inspired by the desire for truth and justice, an idea invented by the troubadours in the 13th Century.

The individual's failing of that "heroic" ideal, due to fear and egotism, exists as a recurring theme in *The Yellow Heart*. Some situations have a sharply satirical edge that indicate Neruda modeled his "hero" on the knight errant, that questing individual who appears mad when viewed through a conventional lens. Often when he refers to such a character in the third person, he is also referring indirectly to his own behavior, in the way others' actions sometimes mirror what we dislike or mistrust about ourselves. He admits to being his own worst enemy or a practitioner of what he accuses others of doing. The satire conforms to Jonathan Swift's description of that tradition as "a sort of glass wherein beholders do generally discover everybody's face but their own, which is the chief reason for the kind of reception it meets in the world, and that so very few are offended with it." However, the poet of *The Yellow Heart* sees his face in the glass, as he does earlier in *Still Another Day* (1969), where he places himself among the *chileanos* who finally conquered the Mapuche in southern Chile after 400 years of warfare. Accepting his true contradictions rather than protecting a false consistency, he no longer includes himself among the victims nor presumes to rescue them from colonization or time. He implicates himself as one who is guilty by association and who, in one aspect or other, fails daily in his mission. Standing in the way of a bicyclist who's rolling down the street

15

in "Morning with Air," the poet attempts to fulfill his hieratic duty by enlightening the shocked bicyclist as to the treachery and murder in the world that most people never see. The arrogant and naive-sounding poet is soon left talking to himself in the street.

Yet, three poems earlier in "Memories of Friendship," the poet disparages his obsessively "selfless" and idealistic friend, Rupertino, for a lifetime of quixotic behavior, while Rupertino fulfills his destiny as *generalisimo* (and resident warmonger) of the tiny country of "Costaragua." The poet tells of his own Sancho-like behavior in accepting a post as military commander and ineffectual adviser to Generalisimo Rupertino, who always had to be right. The dark shades of this allegory, which the poet draws from the history of such countries as Argentina and Brazil, seek the root of the cycle of revolution and dictatorship within the sensibility and character of the individual. His tongue edging into his cheek, the poet tells us:

> He was so stubborn
> my friend, Rupertino,
> he always devoted his unselfish nature
> to futile enterprises:
> he explored explored kingdoms,
> manufactured millions of buttonholes,
> opened a club for heroic widows,
> sold smoke in bottles.
>
> ("Memories of Friendship," *The Yellow Heart*)

In another allegory, "The Hero" is an unnamed nudist with an apartment in the city, who like Rupertino cannot see the paradox of his situation and walls himself in with his fanaticism. When the nudist dies while chasing his canary on the terrace, it finally proves to the poet "that pure faith cannot withstand the assaults of winter."

Among the various shades of parody and humor, Neruda weaves into the fabric numerous omens of mortality and fear that people live with day after day. For him, the primary source of our fear of the world outside lies in our fear of what lies within. In "The Hieroglyphic Chicken," the poet and a friend of his, C.B. (the infamous Charles Baudelaire?), have a third friend who is terrified of the coming of night. The character's exaggerated reaction makes the point that his fear is only objectified as the dusk, an inevitable, non-physical element essential to the cyclical nature of life on earth. The friend tries everything from Buddhism to beer, and even love, to rid himself of his fear of what happens every day as a natural consequence of the planet's turning. In a Parisian restaurant at the crucial hour, the friend throws a dish prepared especially for him at the *maitre d'*, when he sees a terrifying glyph or omen in the food. The fear is of something inside him and not confronted – it is a futile fear, fragmenting his life. Because the Spanish word for chicken, *pollo,* can mean "fellow" or "that guy," there is a suggestion that the friend has become a hieroglyph of himself, a pictograph of his former spirit, mysterious and not completely alive because he will not accept his humanity. (Note that *pollo* in colloquial Spanish does not have the connotation of "coward" or "cowardly" that "chicken" does in English.) This strange and interesting poem, with one of the few slapstick moments in the book, is certainly one that nobody is going to want to see his or her face in.

But there are also lyric poems in the book. "Integrations," for instance, is a beautiful poem celebrating the fact that tenderness is able to exist and that love, in all its fury, persists despite our considerable fear. Underlying Neruda's perspective on fear is the realization that we come to no answers in our emotional and spiritual exploration. The paradox of finding no answers to our questions is an essential condition of being human. In the second poem, "Another," the poet establishes that because he refuses to offer answers, his heart has turned yellow. Neruda frames the paradox in the third-to-last poem:

> One doesn't count illusions
> nor bitter realizations,
> no measure exists to count
> what couldn't happen for us,
> what circled like a bumblebee,

with our not noticing
what we were losing.

> ("Time That Wasn't Lost," *The Yellow Heart*)

However, an elder Neruda takes an explorer's pleasure in life's ambrosia, in this case the delight of falling immodestly in love with a woman and with all of life. In "Love Song," he reaches a new height, orchestrating silliness and tenderness in a mad song:

> On my violin that sings out of tune
> my violin declares,
> I love you, I love you my double bass,
> my sweet woman, dark and clear,
> my heart, my teeth,
> my light and my spoon,
> my salt of the dim week,
> my clear windowpane moon.

> ("Love Song," *The Yellow Heart*)

From the bawdy satires on politics and friendship to the love poems, Neruda's desire to risk alienating readers by once again freeing himself from the "sincere" voice of the politically aware lyric poet probably arose in some part from the circumstances of his life during his final year. One thing is certain about that time: his search for form had its roots deep in an awareness that there is nowhere one can fly "to escape this globe that captured you at birth."

While he was writing *The Yellow Heart,* Neruda maintained a difficult equilibrium among his relationship with his wife, Matilde, as they enjoyed their seaside home in Isla Negra, his struggle with the cancer spreading inside him, and his bitter frustration as he watched conservative Chileans and the military collude with the United States to exploit the political errors of the democratically elected socialist government that had his active support. The poet had recently returned from his post as Ambassador to France, too weakened by disease to complete the task of renegotiating Chile's national debt. While he reconciled himself to his imminent death, Neruda was sifting through a lifetime of possibilities and choices, and was writing shorter, exquisitely crafted books, which he had a better chance of completing than the longer projects more characteristic of his career. It seems that as a mature poet, with the poems coming in more compact and crystalline forms, his vision of the world was clearer than ever.

Neruda's books are always unified in their overall musical structure, each book a series of organic movements that coalesce like a piece of music. This metaphor most closely fits the late and posthumous work, such as *Still Another Day* (1969) and *The Separate Rose* (1973), two long poems of 28 and 24 movements respectively that stand out as symphonic gems. The poems in *The Yellow Heart*, also beautifully orchestrated, range too widely in tone and texture to be organically suited to the tight weave of much of the late work. Their widely fluctuating musical impulses require a looser structure, woven together less by the uniformity of lines than by the dying poet's sensibility and the paradoxical tensions of his world view. His perspective on himself and his passions, as well as various musical strategies, allows for the breadth of the poems. For this reason, it's important to see *The Yellow Heart* in the sweep of his work in order to understand how it accommodates the poet's themes and voices.

Neruda used *Extravagaria* (1958) as a model for the anecdotal and sometimes nonsensical tenor of *The Yellow Heart*. The former launched what critics have called his "autumnal period."

> While things are settling down,
> here I've left my testament,
> my shifting extravagaria,
> so whoever goes on reading it
> will never take in anything
> except the constant moving
> of a clear and bewildered man
> a man rainy and happy,
> lively and autumn-minded.
>
> ("Autumn Testament," *Extravagaria*)

That book was also written during a prolific period and a time of personal change, after the poet (then in his fifties) and Matilde had settled into their relationship and made a home together in Santiago. Neruda had returned from roughly five years of exile in the Soviet Union, Eastern and Western Europe, to an enthusiastic reception in his homeland. *Extravagaria* initiated a poetry of growing personal vulnerability and self-revelation; it also renewed the urgency of the search for new ways of speaking. The roots of the Spanish title, *Extravagario,* can mean eccentric or extravagant, to vary widely or range between opposites, and to be lost or to mislead. These states of mind and metaphorical actions reappear in *The Yellow Heart,* in thematic images and personal symbols that create a correspondence between the two books. This correspondence makes it possible for readers to see, from the earlier book to the later, the typically Nerudian evolution of those images and symbols. Both books present situations in which the poet imagines himself living under the surface of the sea and in which a person makes or fails to make choices amidst the confusions of the day, while unpredictable forces work to shape his destiny. In the earlier book, the poem "Larynx" caricatures the physician as an odd, distant being, more a symbol of mortality than healing. *The Yellow Heart* further develops that theme in a spoof called "I Still Get Around," in which the poet's empirical sense determines that love is a greater healer than modern medicine. But his empirical reasoning and interpretation of experience fall into doubt, pulled by the gravity of life's ultimate question.

> Since then I've never been sure
> whether I should obey
> his decree of death
> or feel as well as my body
> tells me that I do.
>
> And confused, I couldn't decide
> whether to seriously meditate
> or feed myself on carnations.
>
> ("I Still Get Around," *The Yellow Heart*)

The books share corresponding images of camels and hurricanes, tigers and telling lies, but their strongest connection is that they spring in large part from the poet's coming to terms with his mortality.

In *The Yellow Heart,* as in many of the later books, the acceptance of death hinges on the decision to live. The process involves a lifelong dialogue we have with ourselves and with our responses to things that happen every day. But life, like a hurricane or a dog, is always what it is—it never lies. Neruda believes that we alone are responsible for the integrity of our inner dialogue, whether the actions that result are socially unacceptable, impetuously heroic, or futile. Our response to life is shaped by our responses to the moments of clarity we are given, those glimpses of cerulean sky in which truth is migratory. When the inner dialogue is rooted in a world not overly distorted by abstracted fears, understanding and compassion grow inside of us "like tortoises or flowers." When we do not need our arrogance or greed to protect us from the inner or outer world, we come face to face with truth, and our creative energies are renewed.

In the later work, Neruda comes to see himself and others as political, social, and personal beings: all of those lives one life, one responsibility, indivisible from each other. The categories we invent are convenient labels for the mind's machinations, but the person riding a bicycle down the street in "Morning with Air" is all of those beings at the same time. His personal decisions are affected by political decisions, and rolling down the street he is a political force: his personal decisions have political ramifications. Yet, much of the later work, especially *The Yellow Heart,* also confronts the confusion one faces in the daily effort to distinguish between illusion and reality. Neruda admits to confusion in himself and has a good time at his own expense; hand in hand with being subject to life's ambiguities, the poet always keeps a beginner's mind toward his work. Even when reviving a form or cadence he's used in the past, he listens to the current music of the spheres and to his heart as if it were the first time. The past and the present merge in the new poem, as they do in stones and rivers, in all the physical objects of the natural world.

With his beginner's mind, this consummate craftsman retains the sense of wonder he developed as a boy rummaging in the forest. For Neruda, the spiritual world does not exist separately from the physical; they are one in their contradictions and mystery. The spiritual is found in the impurity of stone and the purity of light. It does not exist in words but in silence. In silence, pretension is less likely to undermine the search for spirit in the physical world. Neruda is aware of the irony that lies in his own quest for spiritual regeneration, perhaps because his assaults on silence are often sparked by his sensibility and spirit moving through the natural world. He knows that his poems, strumming their guitars, are moving along with everything else toward silence and light. As James Nolan, the translator of *Stones of the Sky,* put it: "The lesson of stone is that man is only a tentative stage in the millenial dance of matter toward the crystalline light of the emerald or sapphire or ruby: 'the only star that is ours!'" The spiritual binds all matter together. In the human universe the binding agent is love, the way it is memory as well as the moment, casting light and hope into an unforeseen future.

> Close to you is close to me
> and your absence is far from everything
> and the moon is the color of clay
> in the night of quaking earth
> when, in terror of the earth,
> all the roots join together
> and silence is heard ringing
> with the music of fright.
> Fear is also a street.
> And among its terrifying stones
> tenderness somehow is able to march
> with four feet and four lips.
>
> ("Integrations," *The Yellow Heart*)

By loving what and whom we truly love, we continue to transform ourselves and our passion for life. It we allow imagination to run to seed or if our compassion and ability to love perish, we cease to live as full human beings. Instead, we live as sad and willing accomplices in our own demise. To not choose to live is a choice to die.

That was the Ostrogodo family's mistake in "An Untenable Situation," one of Neruda's most deftly handled allegories. The family creates ghosts out of "their respect for the appearances of death," or in other words, out of their fear of living as they sit together all day around the fireplace. They see the ghosts occupying every corner and sitting in every flower vase in the house. When the family flees into the garden, refugees trying to maintain their dignity, the ghosts appear there also. The family's abstracted fears have invaded and occupy their imaginations. The family cannot live with the ghosts because those apparitions embody their greatest fear: to live is also to die. As Neruda says in another poem, their thoughts "remain fixed on a point in the past." They cannot accept themselves or take responsibility for the obsessive projection of fear through which they interpret the present. Those projections take ghostly forms of a nostalgia for life. Much like the protagonists in "Memories of Friendship," "The Hieroglyphic Chicken," and "The Hero," the family members are their own most treacherous enemies. And their dignity, here a catchword for pride, is lost to the dishonesty of the actions meant to secure it.

> And to keep their dignity
> they all went into the garden
> without complaining to the dead,
> a sad cheer on their faces.
>
> ("An Untenable Situation," *The Yellow Heart*)

The model for this poem was "It Happened in Winter" from *Extravagaria*, in which the poet walks through the macabre atmosphere of a deserted house – the holes in the carpet look at him disdainfully and a chair follows him "like a poor lame horse." His imagination animates the furniture and the books, it alters everything, and in the

23

new correspondences between the objects and the poet, nothing is as it was. He flees, having seen what he says he should not have seen: the changing life inside him, an allegory of his death.

> So I never told anyone
> of that visit I didn't make—
> neither does that house exist,
> nor do I know these people,
> nor is this a true story.
>
> ("It Happened in Winter," *Extravagaria*)

Baudelaire's "A Voyage to Cythera" also recalls Neruda's vision of mortality, in one fundamental way. Both in Baudelaire's poem and "An Untenable Situation," the overt and subtle horrors are not found in the presence of death, but in how we see ourselves in relation to Cythera's hanged man or the Ostrogodos' ghosts. In the same measure that this book is indebted to Baudelaire, this poem is a variation on the tradition of *danse macabre*. Death is personified and presented as a sardonic joke. The ghosts, a mirror image of the Ostrogodos' worst fear, drive the family into exile from life. After seeing the hanging corpse, the voyager implores God to help him face his own body without disgust, and the intimidated Ostrogodos indulge their imaginations. As in the poem "Disasters," there is an inescapable parallel between the ghosts invading the house and the cancer invading Neruda's body. Both the ghosts and the cancer were created by the bodies they are destroying. In "Philosophy," Neruda says that we can only hope that "understanding and love come from below." The earth's equation is balanced by the interplay of light and dark, the equinox – any true acceptance of life must also embrace its ending, without allowing death to nest in your heart.

While many of the poems in *The Yellow Heart* address the circumstances of an individual, the final poem "celebrates" the vast communities, or states of mind, called *the suburbs*. In mock-Whitmanesque lines that describe the odd derailment of the pursuit of freedom that the suburbs represent, Neruda includes himself among the middle-class who have purchased the "supreme luxury" of having a full stomach and the illusion of safety, while they wonder who they are and decide what truth is. The poem is a statement of Neruda's dialectical materialism: the price we pay is to work six days a week in "indivisible granaries," where we daily recreate our executioners and the conditions that insidiously enslave us. We retire in the evenings to vast communities built by non-residents, in which residents avoid confronting the realities of life elsewhere. The poem bears witness to what happens when the individual's denial becomes manifest in the character of the community. Vanity, abstracted fear, and the individual's obsession with the biggest and the best break down the relationships that bind the community. (It's likely that is one thing Pinochet hoped to achieve by imposing supply-side commercialism on the Chilean economy: to maintain order and protect his power by replacing social and historical communities with economic ones.) The cycle of getting and spending puts increased emphasis on immediate fulfillment of the selfish wishes and whims and those of the family in its private domain. As we concentrate more upon creating and satisfying the desires of the ego, we lose our moorings in the community, as well as much of our conscious relationship to historical cause and effect. In turn, the loss of historical perspective weakens our feelings of protectiveness toward the culture and our mutual awareness that the well-being of the individual and of the community are one.

Neruda considers it ironic that in the Christian neighborhoods of North and South America, the understanding that what happens to the one happens to the many recedes in our view. One insidious result of this, here and in much of the late work, is greater distance between individuals and families. If something should happen to an individual or family, such as being spirited away in the night as a *desaparecido* or being taken by death, we find ourselves thinking that they must have been different from us in some unspoken and essential way. And, of course, somewhere inside we think it will never happen to us. The poem "Suburbs" suggests that with our self-centered attitudes we tend to experience each other's pain and joy less directly than we might in communities where lives are interwoven on a deeper level. Most days we have difficulty assuming responsibility even for our own actions — we then would have to face the true sources of our limitations and fears. We objectify the reasons we're passed over or forgotten and then blame our oblivion on everybody else:

> because it seems that is the way of the world:
> an endless track of champions
> and in a corner we, forgotten
> maybe because of everybody else,
> since they seemed so much like us
> until they were robbed of the laurels,
> their medals, their titles, their names.

("Suburbs," The Yellow Heart)

When we betray our humanity for the purpose of self-aggrandizement and refuse to see the consequences of our actions, our denial collectively betrays the community. The poet prophesies in "Enigma for the Worried," that only when we die will each of us be granted the "satanic" power to slow down or speed up the hours.

The tension in *The Yellow Heart* is often implicit in the form, as where, in understated language and matter-of-fact tones, the poet presents absurd images such as a person learning to live underwater or taciturn "ghosts" invading a household. Something similar can be seen clearly in the irreverent and tongue-in-cheek poems employing traditional measure and rhyme schemes. The first eleven lines of "Enigma for the Worried" in the original Spanish are among the more interesting examples of this. The strongly iambic rhythm and the richness of the assonant sounds imitate and help to shape the action of the poem, integrating shades of humor with the ennobled and wondrous tone.

Por los días del ano que vendrá
encontraré una hora diferente:
una hora de pelo catarata,
una hora ya nunca transcurrida:
como si el tiempo se rompiera allí
y abriera una ventana: un agujero
por donde deslizarnos hacia el fondo.

Bueno, aquel día con la hora aquella
llegará y dejará todo cambiado:
no se sabrá ya más si ayer se fue
o lo que vuelve es lo que no pasó.

(*"Enigma para intranquilos," The Yellow Heart*)

In its resolve to find "a different hour," the poem moves slowly in the first stanza and against the visual compactness of lines 2–5. The polysyllabic words and the constellation of internal and end rhymes lend regularity to and slow the rhythmic flow, thereby stretching, beyond the visual expectation, the time it takes to speak the lines. The stretching effect exists as a counterpoint to the regularity of the lines, as if seeking an escape from the measurement of time or the finite beating of our hearts. The second stanza answers the movement of the first with visually longer lines, the third and fourth contain series of monosyllabic words that move smoothly and quickly over the tongue. The expectation here is the opposite of what it is in the first stanza. By comparison to the compacted rhythm of the first seven lines, the tenth and eleventh seem almost to evaporate the moment they are spoken, were it not for the accented "o" that brings the stanza to an abrupt end. The lines are suggestive of the elusive and illusive nature of time, translating whatever it touches from an unknown into a known and back again. It constantly slips away from us as we try to orient ourselves within it and escape its grasp. The reader is given no sense of place in the opening lines; the only physical objects are cascading hair and a window that becomes a hole "through which to slide us toward the deep." The measurement of time is what casts illusions of palpability over its passage, its own ephemeral presence separate from human being or physical object. When that presence falls from the clock to the ground, we who think of time as stingy neglect to pick it up! The lack of awareness of passing time is balanced by subtle effects, such as the attempt at prophesy in the first line of the second stanza, with the placement of "that" (*aquel* and *aquella*) before "day" and "hour" to indicate which hour will be the one to leave everything changed in its wake. The more Neruda navigates among paradoxical points of light, the more tongue-in-cheek his perspective:

> For the days of the year to come
> I will find a different hour:
> an hour of cascading hair,
> an hour that never passed:
> as if time were broken there
> and were opening a window: a hole
> through which to slide us toward the deep.
>
> Well, that day that contains that hour
> will arrive and leave everything changed:
> we won't know whether yesterday has passed
> or if what returns is what never happened.
>
>   ("Enigma for the Worried," *The Yellow Heart*)

As in the other Copper Canyon Neruda books, the flow of themes in *The Yellow Heart* circumscribes the motion of the gyre from the first poem to the last. The reader visits various situations in which people wither into their fear, and (as in *Extravagaria*) expectations or plans must be revised due to a new perspective or vision. At regular intervals, the poet craves the integration of humanity with the spiritual purity of the "natural" world, and he celebrates the rejuvenative power and wonder of love. We return over and over to the need for a clear and disciplined reflection on the self, as well as to the need for acceptance of life's events, true understanding, and compassion for human frailty.

The horizontal movement of the book begins with the poet's view of himself as a man woven of women's love and subject to his own weaknesses. He simply followed his passion for playing guitar as he walked through the world, enduring the same threats and absurdities as everybody else. The poet/explorer recalls the time spent living deep inside himself, out of his element as if underwater, while he seeks peace away from the questions that are never asked and that he cannot answer. Allegories that focus on the isolating effects of idealism and abstracted fear are followed by a statement of his "philosophical" belief in the need to live as sensuous beings, enjoying the geography of love, understanding, and ambrosia. The lie of social manners and status is paltry in the face of keeping one's integrity, or of death, in whose eyes we are equal.

Who we are is borne out by how we live, and for Neruda that can be the tender bard driven silly by love or the person who, in his desire to escape the physical and moral entropy of life in a crowded city, emulates a statue. But love insists on keeping things whole, though we are destined to question enigmas and to interpret omens we see in the night sky, in solitude and silence. Learning to do this is a slow process, like loving or dying, and each individual has his own pace at which he comes to face the truth in himself. Whether it's the egomaniacal (yet "selfless") Rupertino who never learns or the evangelical-style poet who stops an unwary bicyclist in the street, we must come to accept loss, the passage of hours, and contradictions in our journey. And yet, we have absolutely nothing to lose: we are a part of a world that has an internal and external balance, night and day, and to defy our nature is not only counterproductive but futile.

The book ends as the poet views the effects of individual frailty on the community. Our denial of the consequences of our actions and inactions can become our executioner, if we do not turn to meet our responsibility. Coming to this realization, the poet wonders how long the beauty of equinox can take to unravel itself, without disrupting the equation of "the world where nothing happens."

The Yellow Heart is the fifth book published in the Copper Canyon Press Late and Posthumous Neruda series in my translation. After the publication of the first book, *Still Another Day,* I chose to translate other volumes published after 1969 that I believe are the strongest and most important to English readers' understanding of Pablo Neruda. The theme of having one more thing to say, introduced in *Still Another Day,* is played off here with poems titled "One," "Another," and "Another One." *The Yellow Heart* continues to develop the movement toward a more personal poetry, as the earlier book does, but spins the expression of it in a very different direction. In both books, Neruda's sharp edge of self-honesty exists side by side with an expanding compassion for others and for himself, and in turn they accompany his clear vision of who he is and what he does in relation to the world.

The Separate Rose, the second book in the series, picks up the theme of the assessment of human temporality and guilt, cast against the mythological and ecological purity of Easter Island. Though he places himself among the tourists who overrun the island with their inability to understand what they are witnessing, he longs to bathe his anguish in the same blue light as the mysterious statues. The return to an ever more personal poetry in the third book, *Winter Garden,* emphasizes nature as a source of spiritual regeneration and embraces solitude as a positive force. That meditation upon death this time establishes the theme of solitude as the state in which we realize the particular character of our humanity. The fourth book, *The Sea and the Bells,* is Neruda's most personal and tightly woven, full-length book of poems since *One Hundred Love Sonnets.* In *The Sea and the Bells,* he links his relationship with Matilde to his love of the cyclic processes of nature, and silence becomes the positive force, a companion to solitude, in its power to help us understand who we are.

In *The Yellow Heart,* the poet continues to include himself in the guilty pathos of humanity, and he embraces solitude and silence. He further evaluates his performance as a poet responsible to his people, another theme that this book shares with the rest of the series. There is another reason, however, that I am publishing this book out of the order Neruda asked his publisher to follow. *The Yellow Heart* seems like a good book with which to honor the poet's request in *Still Another Day* to leave him restless. Neruda did not abide stasis for long in his life or his work, and to understand him is to come to terms with the fact that the only constants in the human world are paradox and change. He avoided saddling his reputation with a typical poem, but kept challenging himself to enter unexplored territory in the search for a greater understanding of his truth. The reader's perception of Neruda will continue to deepen the more he or she reads, a phenomenon that has exhausted his most tenacious translators and critics. *The Yellow Heart* will surprise many longtime readers of Neruda, especially those not familiar with *Extravagaria,* and I hope the book will challenge readers' preconceived or static images of Neruda.

The sixth and last book in the series will be *The Book of Questions* (1974), a book of 74 poems composed entirely of questions (usually one per couplet), which have no rational answers. The book is an exploration of that part of the world we cannot know, with questions that have no answers but that must be pursued in our lifelong journey to find resolution. If we take the journey, though we may never arrive at an answer, we teach ourselves along the way what we need to know in order to love. And in abandoning our inquisitive selves to the process, to the experience that has no answer, we find a greater integration between our imaginations and the circumstances of the planet. When we are aware of and responsive to the complexity and unpredictability of experience, we lead more purposeful lives.

When a translator claims only one Pablo Neruda, he is pressed to illustrate his point. In doing so, I feel somewhat like the knight errant: the expansive nature of Neruda's work has always defied sufficient description in the comparatively narrow parameters of literary criticism. Certainly Neruda, as well as each of his readers, contains "many" selves and voices, as well as the "knowledgeable spirit" that integrates them. He can never really know who he is, nor can we. In his acceptance of his role as a poet and his commitment to the community at large, he asks in *Still Another Day* whether his loneliness died the night he accepted his investiture, or if he was born then, of his solitude? The mature Neruda, the public and the private poet, with his delight in composition and ability to integrate a multiplicity of forms and voices, became like a wheel rolling from its own center.

He writes his own best epitaph in a clear-headed acceptance of mortality, of his growing vulnerability and compassion, which sums up the tenor of his spirit:

> I beg you: leave me restless.
> I live with the impossible ocean
> and silence bleeds me dry
>
> I die with each wave each day.
> I die with each day in each wave.
> But the day does not die.
> Not ever.
> And the wave?
> It does not die.
>
> ("XXVIII," *Still Another Day*)

WILLIAM O'DALY
Winter 1990

THE YELLOW HEART

El corazón amarillo

UNO

Por incompleto y fusiforme
yo me entendí con las agujas
y luego me fueron hilando
sin haber nunca terminado.

Por eso el amor que te doy
mí mujer, mi mujer aguja,
se enrolla en tu oreja mojada
por el vendaval de Chillán
y se desenrolla en tus ojos
desatando melancolías.

No hallo explicación halagüeña
a mi destino intermitente,
mi vanidad me conducía
hacia inauditos heroísmos:
pescar debajo de la arena,
hacer agujeros en el aire,
comerme todas las campanas.
Y sin embargo hice poco
o no hice nada sin embargo,
sino entrar por una guitarra
y salir cantando con ella.

ONE

Because I am unfinished and spindle-shaped
I had an understanding with needles
and then they were threading me
and never have finished.

That's why the love I give you,
my woman, my needle woman,
coils in your ear moistened
by the sea winds of Chillán
and uncoils in your eyes,
letting sadnesses drift.

I don't find pleasant the reasons
my fortune comes and goes,
my vanity escorted me
toward unheard heroics:
to fish beneath the sand,
to make pinholes in air,
to devour every bell.
As it was, I did little
or I did nothing, as it were,
but enter for a guitar
and leave singing with her.

OTRO

De tanto andar una región
que no figuraba en los libros
me acostumbré a las tierras tercas
en que nadie me preguntaba
si me gustaban las lechugas
o si prefería la menta
que devoran los elefantes.
Y de tanto no responder
tengo el corazón amarillo.

ANOTHER

From so often traveling in a region
not charted in books
I grew accustomed to stubborn lands
where nobody ever asked me
whether I like lettuces
or if I prefer mint
like the elephants devour.
And from offering no answers,
I have a yellow heart.

OTRO MAS

Yo volví del fondo del mar
odiando las cosas mojadas:
me sacudí como los perros
de las olas que me querían
y de repente me sentí
contento de mi desembarco
y únicamente terrestre.

Los periodistas dirigieron
su maquinaria extravagante
contra mis ojos y mi ombligo
para que les contara cosas
como si yo me hubiera muerto,
como si yo fuera un vulgar
cadáver especializado,
sin tomar en cuenta mi ser
que me exigía caminar
antes de que yo regresara
a mis costumbres espantosas:
estuve a punto de volver
a sumergirme en la marea.

Porque mi historia se duplica
cuando en mi infancia descubrí
mi depravado corazón
que me hizo caer en el mar
y acostumbrarme a submarino.

Allí estudié para pintor,
allí tuve casa y pescado,

ANOTHER ONE

I returned from the depths of the sea
hating wet things:
like a dog, I shook off
waves that caressed me
and all at once I felt happy
to step back onto land
and utterly of the earth.

The journalists trained
their flamboyant machinery
against my eyes and my navel
to get me to talk with them
as if I were already dead,
as if I were a common
specialized cadaver,
not considering my being
that insisted on walking in the world
before I returned
to my horrendous habits:
I was about to jump
into the ocean again.

The story of my life repeats itself—
as a small child I discovered
my corrupted heart,
which tumbled me into the sea
and accustomed me to life underwater.

There I studied to be a painter,
there I had a house and fish to eat,

bajo las olas me casé,
no me acuerdo ni cuáles fueron
mis novias de profundidad
y lo cierto es que todo aquello
era una incólume rutina:
yo me aburría con los peces
sin incidencias ni batallas
y ellos pensaron que tal vez
yo era un monótono cetáceo.

Cuando por imaginación
pisé la arena de Isla Negra
y viví como todo el mundo,
me tocan tanto la campana
y preguntan cosas idiotas
sobre los aspectos remotos
de una vida tan ordinaria
no sé qué hacer para espantar
a estos extraños preguntones.

Le pido a un sabio que me diga
dónde puedo vivir tranquilo.

I married beneath the waves
but don't remember who they were,
my lovers so many fathoms down,
but it's true that everything fell
into dismal routine:
I got bored of fishes,
no incidents and no battles,
and maybe the fish figured
I was some dull cetacean.

When through my imagination
I step onto the sands of Isla Negra
and live like the rest of the world,
people are ringing the doorbell
to ask idiotic questions
about the obscure facts
of a completely ordinary life,
and I don't know what to do
to frighten off those odd canvassers.

Please, I beg a sage tell me
where I can live in peace.

EL HEROE

En una calle de Santiago
ha vivido un hombre desnudo
por tantos largos años, sí,
sin calzarse, no, sin vestirse
y con sombrero, sin embargo.

Sin más ropaje que sus pelos
este varón filosofante
se mostró en el balcón a veces
y lo vio la ciudadanía
como a un nudista solitario
enemigo de las camisas,
del pantalón y la casaca.

Así pasaban las modas,
se marchitaban los chalecos
y volvían ciertas solapas,
ciertos bastones caídos:
todo era resurrección
y enterramientos en la ropa,
todo, menos aquel mortal
en cueros como vino al mundo,
desdeñoso como los dioses
dedicados a la gimnasia.

(Los testigos y las testigas
del habitante singular
dan detalles que me estremecen
al mostrar la transformación
del hombre y su fisiología.)

THE HERO

On a Santiago street
a naked man lived
for many long years, yes,
without lacing up, no, he never dressed,
but he always wore a hat.

His body clad only in hairs,
this philosophical fellow
appeared at times on the balcony
and the citizens viewed him
as a lonely nudist,
enemy of shirts,
of trousers and overcoats.

So it was, the fashions came and went,
vests withered
and certain lapels returned
certain walking sticks fell:
everything was resurrection
and burials in street clothes,
everything, except that mortal
naked, as he came into the world,
scornful as the patron gods
of athletics.

(The men and women who witnessed
the peculiar neighbor
gave details that shake me
with proof of the transformation
of the man and his physiology.)

Después de aquella desnudez
con cuarenta años de desnudo
desde la cabeza a los pies
se cubrió con escamas negras
y los cabellos le cubrieron
de tal manera los ojos
que nunca pudo leer más,
ni los periódicos del día.

Así quedó su pensamiento
fijo en un punto del pasado
como el antiguo editorial
de un diario desaparecido.

(Curioso caso aquel varón
que murió cuanado perseguía
a su canario en la terraza.)

Queda probado en esta historia
que la buena fe no resiste
las embestidas del invierno.

After all that nudity,
after forty years of being naked
from head to toe,
he was covered with black scales
and long hair covered his eyes
such that he could never read again,
not even the dailies.

In this way, his thoughts remain
fixed on a point in the past,
as on some old editorial
in a defunct newspaper.

(A curious case, that fellow
who died as he was chasing
his canary on the terrace.)

Once again, this story proves
pure faith cannot withstand
the assaults of winter.

Tanto se habló de los difuntos
en la familia de Ostrogodo
que pasó una cosa curiosa,
digna de ser establecida.

Hablaban tanto de los muertos
cerca del fuego todo el día,
del primo Carlos, de Felipe,
de Carlota, monja difunta,
de Candelario sepultado,
en fin, no terminaban nunca
de recordar lo que no vivía.

Entonces en aquella casa
de oscuros patios y naranjos,
en el salón de piano negro,
en los pasillos sepulcrales,
se instalaron muchos difuntos
que se sintieron en su casa.

Lentamente, como ahogados
en los jardines cenicientos
pululaban como murciélagos,
se plegaban como paraguas
para dormir or meditar
y dejaban en los sillones
un olor acre de tumba,

AN UNTENABLE SITUATION

They spoke so often of the dead
in the Ostrogodo family
that a strange thing happened,
one worthy of being recorded.

They used to speak of the dead
all day around the fireplace,
of cousin Carlos, of Felipe,
of Carlota, the deceased nun,
of the entombed Candelario,
in short, they never stopped
recalling who was not alive.

Then, in that house
of dark patios and orange trees,
in the sitting room with the black piano,
in the hallways like crypts,
the many dead settled in
and made themselves at home.

Slowly, like drowned souls
in gardens of ashen light
they swarmed like bats,
they folded like umbrellas
to sleep or to meditate
and left on the armchairs
the acrid odor of a tomb,

un aura que invadió la casa,
un abanico insoportable
de seda color de naufragio.

La familia Ostrogodo apenas
si se atrevía a respirar:
era tan puro su respeto
a los aspectos de la muerte.

Y si aminorados sufrían
nadie les esuchó un susurro.

(Porque hablando de economía
aquella invasión silenciosa
no les gastaba los bolsillos:
los muertos no comen ni fuman,
sin duda esto es satisfactorio:
pero en verdad ocupaban
más y más sitios en la casa.)

Colgaban de los cortinajes,
se sentaban en los floreros,
se disputaban el sillón
de don Filiberto Ostrogodo,
y ocupaban por largo tiempo
el baño, puliendo tal vez
los dientes de sus calaveras:

a soft breeze that invaded the house,
an insufferable silken fan
the color of a shipwreck.

The Ostrogodo family rarely
if ever dared to breathe:
so pure was their respect
for the appearances of death.

And if the dispossessed suffered,
nobody heard a whisper.

(After all, speaking of economics
that silent invasion
didn't cost them a cent:
the dead do not drink or smoke,
and no doubt this was a plus:
but in truth they began to occupy
more and more parts of the house.)

They hung from the draperies,
they sat in flower vases,
they fought over
don Filberto Ostrogodo's easy chair,
and they occupied the bathrooms
for hours, perhaps polishing
the teeth in their skulls:

lo cierto es que aquella familia
fue retirándose del fuego,
del comedor, del dormitorio.
Y conservando su decoro
se fueron todos al jardín
sin protestar de los difuntos,
mostrando una triste alegría.

Bajo la sombra de un naranjo
comían como refugiados
de la frontera peligrosa
de una batalla perdida.
Pero hasta allí llegaron ellos
a colgarse de los ramajes,
serios difuntos circunspectos
que se creían superiores
y no se dignaban hablar
con los benignos Ostrogodos.

Hasta que de tanto morir
ellos se unieron a los otros
enmudeciendo y falleciendo
en aquella casa mortal
que se quedó sin nadie un día
sin puertas, sin casa, sin luz,
sin naranjos y sin difuntos.

the fact is, the family
retreated from the fireplace,
from the dining room, from the beds.
And to keep their dignity
they all went into the garden
without complaining to the dead,
a sad cheer on their faces.

In the shade of an orange tree
they ate like refugees
from the perilous front
of a lost battle.
But even there they came
to hang from the branches,
those serious and circumspect dead
who considered themselves superior
and never stooped to speak
to the goodly Ostrogodos.

Until from all their dying
they joined the others,
becoming silent and passing away
in that mortal house
that one day was left with no inhabitants,
without doors, or house, or light,
without orange trees or the dead.

FILOSOFIA

Queda probada la certeza
del árbol verde en primavera
y de la corteza terrestre:
nos alimentan los planetas
a pesar de las erupciones
y el mar nos ofrece pescados
a pesar de sus maremotos:
somos esclavos de la tierra
que también es dueña del aire.

Paseando por una naranja
me pasé más de una vida
repitiendo el globo terrestre:
la geografía y la ambrosía:
los jugos color de jacinto
y un olor blanco de mujer
como las flores de la harina.

No se saca nada volando
para escaparse de este globo
que te atrapó desde nacer.
Y hay que confesar esperando
que el amor y el entendimiento
vienen de abajo, se levantan
y crecen dentro de nosotros
como cebollas, como encinas,
como galápagos o flores,
como países, como razas,
como caminos y destinos.

PHILOSOPHY

The truth of the green tree
in spring and of Earth's crust
is proven beyond a doubt:
the planets nourish us
despite eruptions
and the sea offers us fish
despite her quaking:
we are slaves of the earth
that is also governess of air.

Walking around an orange
I spent more than one life
echoing the earth's sphere:
geography and ambrosia:
juices the color of hyacinth
and the white scent of woman
like blossoms of flour.

Nothing is gained by flying
to escape this globe
that trapped you at birth.
And we need to confess our hope
that understanding and love
come from below, climb
and grow inside us
like onions, like oak trees,
like tortoises or flowers,
like countries, like races,
like roads and destinations.

De cuando en cuando soy feliz!,
opiné delante de un sabio
que me examinó sin pasión
y me demostró mis errores.

Tal vez no había salvación
para mis dientes averiados,
uno por uno se extraviaron
los pelos de mi cabellera:
mejor era no discutir
sobre mi tráquea cavernosa:
en cuanto al cauce coronario
estaba lleno de advertencias
como el hígado tenebroso
que no me servía de escudo
o este riñón conspirativo.
Y con mi próstata melancólica
y los caprichos de mi uretra
me conducían sin apuro
a un analítico final.

Mirando frente a frente al sabio
sin decidirme a sucumbir
le mostré que podía ver,
palpar, oír y padecer
en otra ocasión favorable.

Y que me dejara el placer
de ser amado y de querer:

I STILL GET AROUND

Now and then, I am happy!,
I stated before a wiseman
who without passion examined me
and pointed out my shortcomings.

Maybe I never found salvation
for my crooked teeth,
each hair on my head
lost its way and fell:
it was better not to argue
the trouble with my cavernous trachea:
as for the rivers in my heart,
they were full of warnings
just as my gloomy liver
that didn't serve as a shield
or this conspiring kidney.
With my saddened prostate
and sudden urges of my urethra,
everything slowly led me
to a final diagnosis.

Staring that sage in the eye
I decided not to succumb
and showed him I was able to see,
to touch, to hear and endure
at the next opportunity.

And so he'd leave me the pleasure
of being loved and of loving:

me buscaría algún amor
por un mes o por una semana
o por un penúltimo día.

El hombre sabio y desdeñoso
me miró con la indiferencia
de los camellos por la luna
y decidió orgullosamente
olvidarse de mi organismo.

Desde entonces no estoy seguro
de si yo debo obedecer
a su decreto de morirme
o si debo sentirme bien
como mi cuerpo me aconseja.

Y en esta duda yo no sé
si dedicarme a meditar
o alimentarme de claveles.

I sought one love or another
for a month or for a week
or for the next-to-last day.

The wise and contemptuous man
watched me with the indifference
that camels have for the moon
and decided in his pride
to forget my entire organism.

Since then I've never been sure
whether I should obey
his decree of death
or feel as well as my body
tells me that I do.

And confused, I couldn't decide
whether to seriously meditate
or feed myself on carnations.

PIEDRAFINA

Debes medirte, caballero,
compañero debes medirte,
me aconsejaron uno a uno,
me aconsejaron poco a poco,
me aconsejaron mucho a mucho,
hasta que me fui desmidiendo
y cada vez me desmedí,
me desmedí cada día
hasta llegar a ser sin duda
horripilante y desmedido,
desmedido a pesar de todo,
inaceptable y desmedido,
desmedidamente dichoso
en mi insurgente desmesura.

Cuando en el río navegable
navegaba como los cisnes
puse en peligro la barcaza
y produje tan grandes olas
con mis estrofas vendavales
que caímos todos al agua.
Allí los peces me miraron
con ojos fríos y reproches
mientras sardónicos cangrejos
amenazaban nuestros culos.

Otra vez asistiendo a un largo,
a un funeral interminable,

PRECIOUS STONE

You must control yourself, sir,
friend, you must control yourself,
they advised me one by one,
they advised me little by little,
they advised me over and over,
until I'd forget myself
and I forgot myself all the time,
I forgot myself every day
until I no doubt became
horrifying and over the edge,
over the edge in spite of it all,
not acceptable and over the edge,
uncontrollably happy
in my rebellious excess.

When on the navigable river
I navigated like the swans,
placing my barge in danger,
and made such huge waves
with my hurricane verses,
we all fell into the water.
There the fish observed me
with cold, reproachful eyes
while sarcastic crayfish
threatened our bottoms.

Another time, assisting at a long,
at an endless funeral,

entre los discursos funestos
me quedé dormido en la tumba
y allí con grave negligencia
me echaron tierra, me enterraron:
durante los días oscuros
me alimenté de las coronas,
de crisantemos putrefactos.
Y cuando resucité
nadie se había dado cuenta.

Con una hermosa me pasó
una aventura desmedida.
Piedrafina, así se llamaba,
se parecía a una cereza,
a un corazón dibujado,
a una cajita de cristal.
Cuando me vio naturalmente
se enamoró de mi nariz,
le prodigó tiernos cuidados
y pequeños besos celestes.

Entonces desencadené
mis inaceptables instintos
y la insaciable vanidad
que me lleva a tantos errores:

between deadly speeches
I remained sleeping in the tomb
and there in an act of grave negligence
they covered me with earth, they buried me:
during those dark days
I fed myself on wreaths
of rotten chrysanthemums.
And when I revived,
nobody had noticed.

I had a fabulous adventure
with a beautiful woman.
Precious Stone, as we called her
she looked like a cherry,
a sketch of a heart,
a small crystal box.
When she saw me, naturally
she was enamored of my nose,
she lavished it gentle caresses
and small celestial kisses.

Then I unchained
my unacceptable urges
and the insatiable vanity
that leads me to so many mistakes:

con esfuerzo desenrollé
mi nariz hasta convertirla
en una trompa de elefante.
Y con mortales malabarismos
llevé a tal grado la destreza
que a Piedrafina levanté
hasta las ramas de un cerezo.

Aquella mujer rechazó
mis homenajes desmedidos
y nunca bajó de las ramas:
me abandonó. Supe después
que poco a poco, con el tiempo,
se convirtió en una cereza.

No hay remedio para estos males
que me hacen feliz tristemente
y amargamente satisfecho:
el orgullo no lleva a nada,
pero la verdad sea dicha:
no se puede vivir sin él.

I struggled to unroll
my nose until it turned
into an elephant's trunk.
With mortal sleights of hand
I took my skill to such a level
that I raised Precious Stone
to the branches of a cherry tree.

That woman rejected
my colossal tributes
and never came down from the branches:
she abandoned me. Afterwards I knew
that little by little, in time,
she turned into a cherry.

There is no remedy for these ills
that have made me sadly joyful
and bitterly satisfied:
pride never gets us anywhere,
but let the truth be spoken:
we cannot live without it.

CANCION DEL AMOR

Te amo, te amo, es mi canción
y aquí comienza el desatino.

Te amo, te amo mi pulmón,
te amo, te amo mi parrón,
y si el amor es como el vino:
eres tú mi predilección
desde las manos a los pies:
eres la copa del después
y la botella del destino.

Te amo al derecho y al revés
y no tengo tono ni tino
para cantarte mi canción,
mi canción que no tiene fin.

En mi violín que desentona
te lo declara mi violín
que te amo, te amo mi violona,
mi mujercita oscura y clara,
mi corazón, mi dentadura,
mi claridad y mi cuchara,
mi sal de la semana oscura,
mi luna de ventana clara.

LOVE SONG

I love you, I love you, is my song
and here my silliness begins.

I love you, I love you my lung,
I love you, I love you my wild grapevine,
and if love is like wine:
you are my predilection
from your hands to your feet:
you are the wineglass of hereafter
and my bottle of destiny.

I love you forwards and backwards,
and I don't have the tone or timbre
to sing you my song,
my endless song.

On my violin that sings out of tune
my violin declares,
I love you, I love you my double bass,
my sweet woman, dark and clear,
my heart, my teeth,
my light and my spoon,
my salt of the dim week,
my clear windowpane moon.

Tanto pasa en el vocerío,
tantas campanas se escucharon
cuando amaban o descubrían
o cuando se condecoraban
que desconfié de la algazara
y me vine a vivir a pie
en esta zona de silencio.

Cuando se cae una ciruela,
cuando una ola se desmaya,
cuando ruedan niñas doradas
en la molicie de la arena,
o cuando una sucesión
de aves inmensas me precede,
en mi callada exploración
no suena ni aúlla ni truena,
no se susurra ni murmulla:
por eso me quedé a vivir
en la música del silencio.

El aire es mudo todavía,
los automóviles resbalan
sobre algodones invisibles
y las muchedumbres políticas
con ademanes enguantados

So much happens in the hubbub,
so many bells were heard to ring
whenever they loved or discovered
or when they decorated each other
that I didn't trust the uproar
and came to live, standing
in this zone of silence.

When a plum falls,
when a wave faints,
when young golden girls roll
on the softness of the sand,
or when in a succession
immense birds guide me –
in my quiet exploration,
it doesn't ring or howl or thunder,
or whisper or murmur:
this is why I live on
in the music of silence.

The air is still mute,
the automobiles skid
on invisible cotton balls
and the political crowds
with gloved gestures

transcurren en un hemisferio
en donde no vuela una mosca.

Las mujeres más parlanchinas
se ahogaron en los estanques
o navegan como los cisnes,
como las nubes en el cielo,
y van los trenes del verano
repletos de frutas y bocas
sin un pitazo ni una rueda
que rechine, como ciclones
encadenados al silencio.

Los meses son como cortinas,
como taciturnas alfombras:
bailan aquí las estaciones
hasta que duerme en el salón
la estatua inmóvil del invierno.

occur in a hemisphere
where no flies buzz.

The most gossipy women
drowned in stone pools
or sail like swans,
like clouds in the sky,
and the summer trains roll
full of fruits and mouths
without a whistle or wheel
that creaks, like cyclones
chained to silence.

The months are like curtains,
like quiet carpets:
here the seasons dance
until it falls asleep in the living room,
the immobile statue of winter.

INTEGRACIONES

Después de todo te amaré
como si fuera siempre antes
como si de tanto esperar
sin que te viera ni llegaras
estuvieras eternamente
respirando cerca de mí.

Cerca de mí con tus costumbres
con tu color y tu guitarra
como están juntos los países
en las lecciones escolares
y dos comarcas se confunden
y hay un río cerca de un río
y dos volcanes crecen juntos.

Cerca de ti es cerca de mí
y lejos de todo es tu ausencia
y es color de arcilla la luna
en la noche del terremoto
cuando en el terror de la tierra
se juntan todas las raíces
y se oye sonar el silencio
con la música del espanto.
El miedo es también un camino.
Y entre sus piedras pavorosas

INTEGRATIONS

After everything, I will love you
as if it were always before,
as if after so much waiting,
not seeing you and you not coming,
you were breathing
close to me forever.

Close to me with your habits
with your color and your guitar
just as countries unite
in schoolroom lectures
and two regions become blurred
and there is a river near a river
and two volcanoes grow together.

Close to you is close to me
and your absence is far from everything
and the moon is the color of clay
in the night of quaking earth
when, in terror of the earth,
all the roots join together
and silence is heard ringing
with the music of fright.
Fear is also a street.
And among its terrifying stones

puede marchar con cuatro pies
y cuatro labios, la ternura.

Porque sin salir del presente
que es un anillo delicado
tocamos la arena de ayer
y en el mar enseña el amor
un arrebato repetido.

tenderness somehow is able to march
with four feet and four lips.

Since, without leaving the present
that is a fragile ring,
we touch the sand of yesterday
and on the sea, love reveals
a repeated fury.

GATOS NOCTURNOS

Cuántas estrellas tiene un gato
me preguntaron en París
y comencé tigre por tigre
a acechar las constelaciones:
porque dos ojos acechantes
son palpitaciones de Dios
en los ojos fríos del gato
y dos centellas en el tigre.

Pero es una estrella la cola
de un gato erizado en el cielo
y es un tigre de piedra azul
la noche azul de Antofagasta.

La noche gris de Antofagasta
se eleva sobre las esquinas
como una derrota elevada
sobre la fatiga terrestre
y se sabe que es el desierto
el otro rostro de la noche
tan infinita, inexplorada
como el no ser de las estrellas.

Y entre las dos copas del alma
los minerales centellean.

Nunca vi un gato en el desierto:
la verdad es que nunca tuve

NIGHT CATS

A cat has how many stars,
they asked me in Paris,
and I, tiger by tiger, began
to observe the constellations:
because two watching eyes
are pulsations of God
in the cat's cold eyes
and two lightning bolts in the tiger's.

But a star is the tail
of a cat bristled in the sky
and a blue stone tiger is
blue night of Antofagasta.

Gray night of Antofagasta
rose over the corners
like a lofty defeat
over earth's exhaustion
and it's a fact, the desert
is the other face of night,
so infinite, unexplored,
like the non-existence of the stars.

And between two goblets of the soul
the minerals sparkle.

I never saw a cat in the desert:
but the truth is, I never

para dormir más compañía
que las arenas de la noche,
las circunstancias del desierto
o las estrellas del espacio.

Porque así no son y así son
mis pobres averiguaciones.

slept with anybody
but the sands of night,
the circumstances of the desert
or the stars in space.

Because they aren't and they are
my humble discoveries.

Centella, tú me dedicaste
la lentitud de mis trabajos:
con la advertencia equinoccial
de tu fosfórica amenaza
yo recogí mis preferencias,
renuncié a lo que no tenía
y encontré a mis pies y a mis ojos
las abundancias del otoño.

Me enseñó el rayo a ser tranquilo,
a no perder luz en el cielo,
a buscar adentro de mí
las galerías de la tierra,
a cavar en el suelo duro
hasta encontrar en la dureza
el mismo sitio que buscaba,
agonizando, el meteoro.

Aprendí la velocidad
para dejarla en el espacio
y de mi lento movimiento
hice una escuela innecesaria
como una tertulia de peces
cuyo paseo cotidiano
se desarrolla entre amenazas.

REJECT THE LIGHTNING

Lightning, you committed me
to the slow pace of my work:
with the warning at equinox
of your phosphoric threat
I gathered up my choices,
renounced what wasn't mine
and found at my feet and with my eyes
the abundances of autumn.

The flash taught me to be calm,
not to lose light in the sky,
to search inside of myself
for the galleries of Earth,
to dig in the hard ground
until finding in that hardness
the same site, in its agony,
the meteor was seeking.

I learned the velocity
needed to leave it in space,
and to study my slowness
I formed a frivolous school
like a coterie of fishes
whose daily glide and turn
develops between threats.

Este es el estilo de abajo,
del manifiesto submarino.

Y no lo pienso desdeñar
por una ley de la centella:
cada uno con su señal,
con lo que tuvo en este mundo,
y me remito a mi verdad
porque me falta una mentira.

This is the style of down below,
of the manifesto under the sea.

And I do not believe that I'll ignore it
because of some damned law:
each with its flashing signal,
with what it had in the world,
and I turn toward my truth
because I am lacking a lie.

DESASTRES

Cuando llegué a Curacautin
estaba lloviendo ceniza
por voluntad de los volcanes.

Me tuve que mudar a Talca
donde habían crecido tanto
los ríos tranquilos de Maule
que me dormí·en una embarcación
y me fui a Valparaíso.

En Valparaíso caían
alrededor de mí las casas
y desayuné en los escombros
de mi perdida biblioteca
entre un Baudelaire sobrevivo
y un Cervantes desmantelado.

En Santiago las elecciones
me expulsaron de la ciudad:
todos se escupían la cara
y a juzgar por los periodistas
en el cielo estaban los justos
y en la calle los asesinos.

Hice mi cama junto a un río
que llevaba más piedras que agua,

DISASTERS

When I arrived in Curacautin
it was raining ash
because the volcanoes willed it.

I had to detour to Talca
where they had grown so wide,
those tranquil rivers of Maule,
that I fell asleep on a boat
and went to Valparaíso.

In Valparaíso the houses
were falling around me
and I ate breakfast in the wreckage
of my lost library
between a surviving Baudelaire
and a dismantled Cervantes.

In Santiago the elections
expelled me from the city:
everybody spit in each other's faces
and according to the reporters,
the righteous were in the sky,
and in the streets, assassins.

I made my bed next to a river
that carried more stones than water,

junto a unas encinas serenas,
lejos de todas las ciudades,
junto a las piedras que cantaban
y al fin pude dormir en paz
con cierto temor de una estrella
que me miraba y parpadeaba
con cierta insistencia maligna.

Pero la mañana gentil
pintó de azul la noche negra
y las estrellas enemigas
fueron tragadas por la luz
mientras yo cantaba tranquilo
sin catástrofe y sin guitarra.

next to some serene oaks,
far from every city,
next to stones that were singing,
and finally I was able to sleep in peace
in certain terror of a star
that was watching me and winking
with a certain malignant insistence.

But the gentle morning
painted the black night blue
and the enemy stars
were swallowed by light
while I sang peacefully
with no catastrophe and no guitar.

Era una tal obstinación
la de mi amigo Rupertino
que empeñó su desinterés
en siempre inútiles empresas:
exploró reinos explorados,
fabricó millones de ojales,
abrió un club de viudas heroicas
y vendía el humo en botellas.

Yo desde niño hice de Sancho
contra mi socio quijotesco:
alegué con fuerza y cordura
como una tía protectora
cuando quiso plantar naranjos
en los techos de Notre-Dame.
Luego, cansado de sufrirlo,
lo dejé en una nueva industria:
"Bote Ataúd", "Lancha Sarcófago"
para presuntos suicidas:
mi paciencia no pudo más
y le corté mi vecindad.

Cuando mi amigo fue elegido
Presidente de Costaragua
me designó Generalísimo,
a cargo de su territorio:
era su orden invadir
las monarquías cafeteras
regidas por reyes rabiosos
que amenazaban su existencia.

MEMORIES OF FRIENDSHIP

He was so stubborn
my friend Rupertino,
he always devoted his unselfish nature
to futile enterprises:
he explored explored kingdoms,
manufactured millions of buttonholes,
opened a club for heroic widows
and sold smoke in bottles.

From childhood I was Sancho
to my quixotic partner:
I argued with force and good sense
like a protective aunt
when he wanted to plant orange trees
on the roofs of Notre Dame.
Then, finding him insufferable,
I left him to a new industry:
"Coffin Boats," "Motorboat Sarcophagi,"
for presumed suicides:
my patience was spent
and I cut him out of my life.

When my friend was elected
President of Costaragua
he made me *generalisimo*
in charge of his territories:
he ordered me to invade
the coffeepot monarchies
governed by rabid kings
who threatened his existence.

Por debilidad de carácter
y amistad antigua y pueril
acepté aquellas charreteras
y con cuarenta involuntarios
avancé sobre las fronteras.

Nadie sabe lo que es morder
el polvo de la derrota:
entre Marfil y Costaragua
se derritieron de calor
mis aguerridos combatientes
y me quedé solo, cercado
por cincuenta reyes rabiosos.

Volví contrito de las guerras:
sin título de General.
Busqué a mi amigo quijotero:
nadie sabía dónde estaba.

Lo encontré luego en Canadá
vendiendo plumas de pingüino
(ave implume por excelencia)
(lo que no tenía importancia
para mi compadre obstinado).

El día menos pensado
puede aparecer en su casa:
créale todo lo que cuenta
porque después de todo es él
el que siempre tuvo razón.

Out of a weakness of character
and old and childish friendship
I accepted some sashes with medals
and with forty unwilling volunteers
I advanced across the borders.

Nobody knows what it is to swallow
the dust of defeat:
between Marfil and Costaragua,
my combat-hardened troops
melted in the heat
and I alone was left, fenced in
by fifty rabid kings.

I returned contrite from the wars:
stripped of the title of General.
I searched for my quixotic friend:
nobody knew where he was.

Later, I found him in Canada
selling penguin feathers
(loveliest of featherless birds)
(which held no importance at all
for my single-minded companion).

The day you least expect it,
he may appear on your doorstep:
believe everything he tells you
because after all is said and done
he's the one who was always right.

ENIGMA PARA INTRANQUILOS

Por los días del año que vendrá
encontraré una hora diferente:
una hora de pelo catarata,
una hora ya nunca transcurrida:
como si el tiempo se rompiera allí
y abriera una ventana: un agujero
por donde deslizarnos hacia el fondo.

Bueno, aquel día con la hora aquella
llegará y dejará todo cambiado:
no se sabrá ya más si ayer se fue
o lo que vuelve es lo que no pasó.

Cuando de aquel reloj caiga una hora
al suelo, sin que nadie la recoja,
y al fin tengamos amarrado el tiempo,
ay! sabremos por fin dónde comienzan
o dónde se terminan los destinos,
porque en el trozo muerto o apagado
veremos la materia de las horas
como se ve la pata de un insecto.

Y dispondremos de un poder satánico:
volver atrás o acelerar las horas:
llegar al nacimiento o a la muerte
como un motor robado al infinito.

ENIGMA FOR THE WORRIED

For the days of the year to come
I will find a different hour:
an hour of cascading hair,
an hour that never passed:
as if time were broken there
and were opening a window: a hole
through which to slide us toward the deep.

Well, that day that contains that hour
will arrive and leave everything changed:
we won't know whether yesterday has passed
or if what returns is what never happened.

When an hour falls from that clock
to the ground and nobody picks it up,
and at last we have time tied up,
O! we finally will know where our destinies
begin and where they end
because in the dead or extinguished fragment
we will see what composes the hours
as clearly as we view the leg of an insect.

And we will possess a satanic power:
to turn back or speed up the hours:
to arrive at birth or at death
like an engine stolen from the infinite.

Tan defectuoso era mi amigo
que no soportaba el crepúsculo.
Era una injuria personal
la aproximación de la sombra,
la duda crítica del día.

Mi pobre amigo aunque heredero
de posesiones terrenales
podía cambiar de estación
buscando el país de la nieve
o las palmeras de Sumatra:
pero, cómo evitarle al día
el crepúsculo inevitable?

Intentó somníferos verdes
y alcoholes extravagantes,
nadó en espuma de cerveza,
acudió a médicos, leyó
farmacopeas y almanaques:
escogió el amor a esa hora,
pero todo resultó inútil:
casi dejaba de latir
o palpitaba demasiado
su corazón que rechazaba
el advenimiento fatal
del crepúsculo de cada día.

Penosa vida que arrastró
mi amigo desinteresado.

THE HIEROGLYPHIC CHICKEN

My friend was so messed up
he could not bear the last light.
He felt the closeness of shadow
like a physical wound,
that crucial question of the day.

Although my poor friend was heir
to material possessions,
he was able to change seasons,
seeking out the snow country
or the palm trees of Sumatra:
but every day, how to avoid
the inevitable dusk?

He tried green sleeping pills
and extravagant liquors,
he swam in beer foam,
he called on doctors, read
pharmacopoeias and almanacs:
in that hour he chose love,
but everything proved futile:
his heart would almost stop
or beat too rapidly
when it fought off
the deadly arrival
of each day's dusk.

Behind him, my numb friend
dragged a shameful life.

Con C. B. íbamos con él
a un restaurante de París
a esa hora para que se viera
la aproximación de la noche.
Nuestro amigo creyó encontrar
un jeroglífico inquietante
en un manjar que le ofrecían.
Y acto seguido, iracundo,
arrojó el pollo jeroglífico
a la cabeza del benigno
maître d'hôtel del restaurante.
Mientras se cerraba el crepúsculo
como un abanico celeste
sobre las torres de París,
la salsa bajaba a los ojos
del servidor desorientado.

Llegó la noche y otro día
y sobre nuestro atormentado,
qué hacer? Cayó el olvido oscuro
como un crepúsculo de plomo.

C. B. me recuerda esta historia
en una carta que conservo.

C.B. and I went with him
to a restaurant in Paris
at the hour he would encounter
the approach of night.
Our friend was convinced he'd find
an unsettling hieroglyph
in a dish they were offering him.
And immediately after, in a rage,
he threw the hieroglyphic chicken
at the head of the restaurant's
good-hearted *maitre d'*.
While dusk was closing
like a celestial fan
over the towers of Paris,
the sauce was running into the eyes
of the disoriented waiter.

Night arrived and another day
and about our tormented friend,
what to do? Dark oblivion fell
like a leaden dusk.

C.B. recalled this story
in a letter that I saved.

MAÑANA CON AIRE

Del aire libre prisionero
va un hombre a media mañana
como un globo de cristal.
Qué puede saber y conocer
si está encerrado como un pez
entre el espacio y el silencio,
si los follajes inocentes
le esconden las moscas del mal?

Es mi deber de sacerdote,
de geógrafo arrepentido,
de naturalista engañado,
abrir los ojos del viajero:

Me paro en medio del camino
y detengo su bicicleta:

Olvidas, le digo, villano,
ignorante lleno de oxígeno,
el tugurio de las desdichas
y los rincones humillados?

Ignoras que allí con puñal,
acá con garrote y pedrada,
más allá con revólver negro
y en Chicago con tenedor

MORNING WITH AIR

Prisoner of the outdoors,
a man rolls by at mid-morning
like a crystalline globe.
What can he understand or know
if he's caught like a fish
between space and silence,
if innocent bushes
hide flies of evil from him?

It is my duty as a priest,
as a penitent geographer,
as a swindled naturalist,
to open the traveler's eyes:

I halt in the middle of the street
and stop his bicycle:

Have you forgotten, I ask him, villain,
know-nothing full of oxygen,
the hovel of misfortune
and the humiliated corners?

You ignore that, there with a dagger,
here with a club and a thrown stone,
farther away with a black revolver
and in Chicago with a fork

se asesinan las alimañas,
se despedazan las palomas
y se degüellan las sandías?

Arrepiéntete del oxígeno,
dije al viajero sorprendido,
no hay derecho a entregar la vida
a la exclusiva transparencia.

Hay que entrar en la casa oscura,
en el callejón de la muerte,
tocar la sangre y el terror,
compartir el mal espantoso.

El transeúnte me clavó
sus dos ojos incomprensivos
y se alejó en la luz del sol
sin responder ni comprender.

Y me dejó — triste de mí —
hablando solo en el camino.

vermin are assassinated,
doves are torn apart
and watermelons have their throats cut?

Be ashamed of oxygen,
I told the surprised traveler,
nobody has the right to surrender his life
to one single clarity.

We need to enter the dark house,
the alley of death,
to touch the blood and the terror,
to share the horrific evil.

The wanderer nailed me
with his two confused eyes
and he moved away in the sunlight
without responding or understanding.

And he left me – poor me –
talking to myself in the street.

EL TIEMPO QUE NO SE PERDIO

No se cuentan las ilusiones
ni las comprensiones amargas,
no hay medida para contar
lo que no podría pasarnos,
lo que rondó como abejorro
sin que no nos diéramos cuenta
de lo que estábamos perdiendo.

Perder hasta perder la vida
es vivir la vida y la muerte
y no son cosas pasajeras
sino constantes evidentes
la continuidad del vacío,
el silencio en que cae todo
y por fin nosotros caemos.

Ay! lo que estuvo tan cerca
sin que pudiéramos saber.
Ay! lo que no podía ser
cuando tal vez podía ser.

Tantas alas circunvolaron
las montañas de la tristeza
y tantas ruedas sacudieron
la carretera del destino
que ya no hay nada que perder.

Se terminaron los lamentos.

TIME THAT WASN'T LOST

One doesn't count illusions
nor bitter realizations,
no measure exists to count
what couldn't happen for us,
what circled like a bumblebee,
without our not noticing
what we were losing.

To lose until we lose our life
is to live our life and our death,
and nothing that passes on exists
that doesn't give constant proof
of the continuous emptiness of all,
the silence into which everything falls
and, finally, we fall.

O! what came so close
that we were never able to know.
O! what was never able to be
that maybe could have been.

So many wings flew around
the mountains of sorrow
and so many wheels beat
the highway of our destiny,
we had nothing left to lose.

And our weeping ended.

OTRA COSA

Me suceden tan pocas cosas
que debo contar y contarlas.
Nadie me regala asfodelos
y nadie me hace suspirar.
Porque llegué a la encrucijada
de un enrevesado destino
cuando se apagan los relojes
y cae el cielo sobre el cielo
hasta que el día moribundo
saca a la luna de paseo.

Hasta cuándo se desenreda
esta belleza equinoccial
que de verde pasa a redonda,
de ola marina a catarata,
de sol soberbio a luna blanca,
de soledad a capitolio,
sin que se altere la ecuación
del mundo en que no pasa nada?

No pasa nada sino un día
que como ejemplar estudiante
se sienta con sus galardones
detrás de otro día premiado,
hasta que el coro semanal
se ha convertido en un anillo

ANOTHER THING

So little happens to me
that I must count and recount.
Nobody gives me asphodels
and nobody makes me sigh.
Because I arrived at the crossroads
from a complicated destination,
when ticking clocks fade away
and the sky tumbles across the sky
until the dying day
takes the moon for a walk.

How long does the beauty of equinox
take to disentangle itself,
turning from green to round,
from ocean wave to cataract,
from proud sun to white moon,
from solitude to capital city,
without changing the equation
of the world where nothing happens.

Nothing happens except a day
that like a model student
weighs its worth in rewards
at the end of another winning day,
until the once-a-week chorus
has turned itself into a ring

que ni la noche transfigura
porque llega tan alhajada,
tan portentosa como siempre.

A ver si pescan peces locos
que trepen como ornitorrincos
por las paredes de mi casa
y rompan el nuevo equilibrio
que me persigue y me atormenta.

that not even night transfigures
because it arrives encrusted with jewels,
full of omens as always.

Let's see if they can net the crazy fish
that climb like platypuses
along the walls of my house
and shatter the new harmony
that pursues me and torments me.

SUBURBIOS

Celebro las virtudes y los vicios
de pequeños burgueses suburbanos
que sobrepasan el refrigerador
y colocan sombrillas de color
junto al jardín que anhela una piscina:
este ideal del lujo soberano
para mi hermano pequeño burgués
que eres tú y que soy yo, vamos diciendo
la verdad verdadera en este mundo.

La verdad de aquel sueño a corto plazo
sin oficina el sábado, por fin,
lost despiadados jefes que produce
el hombre en los graneros insolubles
donde siempre nacieron los verdugos
que crecen y se multiplican siempre.

Nosotros, héroes y pobres diablos,
débiles, fanfarrones, inconclusos,
y capaces de todo lo imposible
siempre que no se vea ni se oiga,
donjuanes y donjuanas pasajeros
en la fugacidad de un corredor
o de un tímido hotel de pasajeros.
Nosotros con pequeñas vanidades
y resistidas ganas de subir,
de llegar donde todos han llegado
porque así nos parece que es el mundo:

SUBURBS

_____

I celebrate the virtues and vices
of suburban middle-class people
who overwhelm the refrigerator
and position colorful umbrellas
near the garden that longs for a pool:
for my middle-class brother
this principle of supreme luxury:
what are you and what am I, and we go on deciding
the real truth in this world.

The truth of that dream we buy on credit
of not going to the office on Saturday, at last,
and the merciless bosses whom the worker
manufactures in indivisible granaries
where executioners were always born
and grow up and always multiply.

We, heroes and poor devils,
the feeble, the braggarts, the unfinished,
and capable of everything impossible
as long as it's not seen or heard,
Don Juans, women and men, who come and go
with the fleeting passage of a runner
or of a shy hotel for travelers.
And we with our small vanities,
our controlled hunger for climbing
and getting as far as everybody else has gotten
because it seems that is the way of the world:

una pista infinita de campeones
y en un rincón nosotros, olvidados
por culpa de tal vez todos los otros
porque eran tan parecidos a nosotros
hasta que se robaron sus laureles,
sus medallas, sus títulos, sus nombres.

an endless track of champions
and in a corner we, forgotten
maybe because of everybody else,
since they seemed so much like us
until they were robbed of their laurels,
their medals, their titles, their names.

ABOUT THE TRANSLATOR

William O'Daly has been translating Neruda's poetry for the last fifteen years. He has published four other books of Neruda translations with Copper Canyon Press, as well as a chapbook of his own poems, *The Whale in the Web*. He currently works as a technical editor for the Microsoft Corporation and teaches as an adjunct faculty member at Antioch University Seattle.